Voices from the American Revolution

SOLDIERS

David Haugen, Book Editor

BLACKBIRCH®
PRESS

THOMSON

GALE

San Diego • Detroit • New York • San Francisco • Cleveland • New Haven, Conn. • Waterville, Maine • London • Munich

THOMSON
✳
™
GALE

<u>LIBRARY OF CONGRESS CATALOGING-IN-PUBLICATION DATA</u>
Soldiers / by David Haugen
    p. cm. — (Voices from the American Revolution)
Summary: A history of the Revolutionary War, as told through diary excerpts, letters,
and personal narratives from soldiers, military leaders, medical personnel, and other
combat eyewitnesses.
Includes bibliographical references. (p.) and index.
  ISBN 1-56711-956-5 (lib. bdg. : alk. paper)
  1. United States—History—Revolution, 1775–1783—Personal narratives—Juvenile
literature. 2. Soldiers—United States—Biography—Juvenile literature. 3. Soldiers—Great
Britain—Biography—Juvenile literature. 4. United States. Continental Army—Biography—
Juvenile literature. 5. Great Britain. Army—Biography—Juvenile literature. [1. United
States—History—Revolution, 1775–1783—Personal narratives. 2. Soldiers] I. Haugen,
David M., 1969– II. Series.

E275.A2S65 2004
973.3'3'0922—dc22
                                        2003062991

CONTENTS

THE MEN WHO FOUGHT THE REVOLUTION

On April 19, 1775, American minutemen assembled on the green at Lexington, Massachusetts, to block the passage of British troops on their way to the nearby town of Concord. In the early morning hours, the British marched into Lexington and, seeing the armed colonials, arrayed themselves in a battle line. After the British commander ordered the colonial minutemen to disperse, a shot rang out from some unknown location, and the two sides began to fight. The war of the Revolution had begun.

Although the skirmish on the Lexington green may seem to stand out from the many battles fought between the British and the colonial forces from 1775 to 1783, it possessed many of the traits that characterized most of the combat during the Revolution. The British soldiers were part of a professional army. Common infantry soldiers were splendidly attired in white uniforms covered by scarlet coats. They were well disciplined, and leaders could maneuver their regiments with ease.

In combat, the British infantry fought in a line formation—multiple rows of soldiers would line up and face off against an enemy roughly one hundred yards away. The distance was determined by the effective range of the brown Bess musket that was standard issue to each soldier. A successful volley of musket fire was often followed by a bayonet charge in which each soldier would fix a bayonet—or long metal blade—to the end of his musket and charge with the rest of his line toward the enemy. The charge was frightening to an inexperienced enemy and usually resulted in instant flight.

Standing across the Lexington green from the British was the colonial militia. This group of patriot citizens was not part of a national, professional army. Each town typically raised its own militia units from the local residents who owned firearms. These men, who could range in age from sixteen to seventy, assembled regularly to practice marching and firing. Their leaders may have had experience fighting against Native

Minutemen, like the one pictured here, were patriotic residents of New England towns who were ready to fight at a moment's notice.

Hessian mercenaries (right), who were well equipped with uniforms, muskets, and bayonets, joined British soldiers to fight colonial forces.

Americans or they may have been veterans of the French and Indian War (1755–1763). Quite often, however, militia leaders were inexperienced fighters who held their leadership positions simply because they were prominent in their communities. The militia captain may have kept a uniform from the French and Indian War, but most likely he and his men dressed in hunting clothes or whatever other garments they could muster. They carried a variety of weapons from flintlock pistols to hunting rifles to tomahawks. No one owned a bayonet.

The militia companies made up the largest part of the colonial army throughout the Revolution. Many distinguished themselves in battle, but too often they fired one volley and then fled from the intimidating British line infantry. George Washington and other American commanders criticized the militia for their cowardice and their unwillingness to serve through long campaigns. Since militiamen were also farmers and small businessmen, they periodically abandoned the army and returned to their fields and stores to keep their livelihoods afloat.

Militia units were not the only colonial forces to take part in the war. Just after the Battles of Lexington and Concord, the Continental Congress approved the creation of a Continental army and appointed George Washington to lead it. The Continental army was to be a national force composed of soldiers from each colony who would be committed to lengthy terms of enlistment. Since the colonies put together their own regiments, the Continental army still was not as unified as the British army. Before 1779, the army had no official uniform, and the Congress could rarely afford standard-issue equipment.

Furthermore, although the Congress called for an army of around twenty thousand men, Washington faced his first campaigns with less than half that number. Even as the years of fighting wore on and Congress raised the enlistment figure to eighty thousand, the Continental army rarely exceeded fifteen thousand men. Despite the handicap, the Continentals had excellent commanders, and the training of the average foot soldier was nearly equal to that of the British. For this reason, the presence of Continentals in a battle often helped the colonials withstand well-executed British attacks.

The task of training the Continental army was given to foreign military men who favored the American cause and volunteered to take part in the fight. The most well-known of these was a Prussian soldier of fortune named Friedrich von Steuben. He began a regimented instruction of the Continental army at its winter quarters at Valley Forge in 1777. Under von Steuben's guidance, the Continental army became more disciplined, and it learned to fight like the British and the other armies of Europe.

Other foreign volunteers greatly aided the patriot cause. The most notable were the French, who sent volunteer officers to help lead and train the new army as early as 1776. Perhaps more important, the French sent muskets, bayonets, cannons, and standard-issue uniforms to help meld the Continental army into a unified and effective fighting force. The French officially joined the war in 1778. It was not until 1780, however, that French troops landed in America. These six thousand professional soldiers were instrumental in helping George Washington defeat the British army at Yorktown—the last major battle of the Revolution.

The British also had foreign allies. To bolster its troop strength in the colonies, the British Crown hired mercenaries from various German principalities. The majority (seventeen thousand) came from Hesse-Cassel, giving rise in the colonies to the term Hessians to describe all of the German adversaries. These men had a lot of experience fighting European wars, and they proved to be a valuable asset to the British, who found it cheaper to hire their services than to recruit more British troops.

British forces were also reinforced by loyalist militias in the colonies, several Native American tribes, and black slaves who preferred military service to enslavement at the hands of the colonists. Many African Americans also fought on the side of the patriots. Several were freemen, and some were slaves who joined the ranks alongside their masters. Some of these slaves also were sent alone into the Continental army, since white men could forgo military enlistment by sending another person in their place. With all of these various participants, the Revolution became by war's end a truly multicultural and multinational event—quite different in character than was suggested by the two sides that faced off on the Lexington green in April 1775.

CHRONOLOGY OF THE REVOLUTION

MARCH 1765

King George III of England approves the Stamp Act, which taxes the American colonies to help pay for the French and Indian War. Colonists protest the tax as unfair because it was levied without colonial representation in Parliament.

AUGUST 1768

Boston firebrand Samuel Adams calls for a boycott of English imports. In response, England sends troops to the colonies to maintain order.

MARCH 1770

Five colonists are killed after a brief confrontation with British soldiers outside Boston's Customs House. Known as the Boston Massacre, the event adds to the tensions in the colonies.

SEPTEMBER 1774

The colonies send delegates to the First Continental Congress to address the tensions between England and America.

JULY 1776

The Continental Congress votes to declare American independence. It adopts Thomas Jefferson's Declaration of Independence as its testimonial of British abuses and American resolve to be free.

DECEMBER 1776

Washington stages a daring surprise attack on Trenton, New Jersey, where Hessian mercenaries working for the British have camped for the winter.

OCTOBER 1777

While Washington fights battles in Pennsylvania, General Horatio Gates achieves a resounding victory over British general John Burgoyne's army near Saratoga, New York. Burgoyne's army is the first British command to surrender to patriot forces.

King George III of England

APRIL–AUGUST 1775

- The British commander in Boston sends units to nearby Lexington and Concord to seize colonial weapons and ammunition. The colonists are alerted to his move, and militia units from neighboring colonies converge on Concord to stop the British advance. The two sides exchange fire, and the British are forced to retreat back to Boston.

- The Continental Congress meets again to discuss breaking free from English rule. It appoints George Washington as the commander of military forces in America.

- Before Washington can arrive to take charge of the patriot units around Boston, the British advance and achieve a costly victory at the Battle of Bunker Hill.

- In August, after finally hearing of the skirmish at Lexington and Concord, King George III declares the colonies to be in revolt.

FEBRUARY 1778–JUNE 1779

- Benjamin Franklin helps broker a formal military alliance between France and America.

- France declares war on England.

- Spain officially declares war on England.

JULY–OCTOBER 1781

French troops arrive in Rhode Island. Their commander, the Comte de Rochambeau, persuades Washington to stage an offensive in the South against British forces under Lord Charles Cornwallis. With the French fleet cutting off Cornwallis's retreat by sea, the combined American and French armies surround the British army at Yorktown, Virginia, and force Cornwallis to surrender on October 19.

SEPTEMBER 1783

The Treaty of Paris is signed and the war ends, despite the fact that the Continental Congress would not finish ratifying the treaty until the following year. In November, George Washington resigns his commission as head of the Continental army.

George Washington

Facing the British at Concord

On the morning of April 19, 1775, a small band of colonial militia barred the advance of a column of British troops marching through Lexington, Massachusetts. As the two sides faced off on the town's green, the British soldiers fired into the colonists, killing eight men and forcing the others to flee. The British continued their march to the neighboring town of Concord. When the British reached Concord, they found that a larger group of militia awaited them. Colonial soldiers had poured into Concord from the surrounding countryside. One of these men was Amos Barrett, a Concord native. Barrett and the militia then gave chase as the British retreated through Concord and back toward Lexington.

Glossary

- **all of his mind:** in agreement with him
- **waylaid:** ambushed

We at Concord heard they was a-coming. The Bell rung at 3 o'clock for an alarm. As I was then a Minuteman, I was soon in town and found my captain and the rest of my company at the post. It wasn't long before there was other minute companies. One company, I believe, of minutemen was raised in almost every town to stand at a minute's warning. Before sunrise there was, I believe, 150 of us and more of all that was there. . . .

When we was on the hill by the bridge, there was about eighty or ninety British came to the bridge and there made a halt. After a while they begun to tear up the plank of the bridge. Major Buttrick said if we were all of his mind, he would drive them away from the bridge; they should not tear that up. We all said we would go. We then wasn't loaded; we were all ordered to load—and had strict orders not to fire till they fired first, then to fire as fast as we could. . . .

They stayed about ten minutes and then marched back, and we after them. After a while we found them a-marching back towards Boston. We was soon after them. When they got about a mile and a half to a road that comes from Bedford and Billerica, they was waylaid and a great many killed. When I got there, a great many lay dead and the road was bloody.

Amos Barrett, account of the Battle of Concord, ca. 1775.

FREDERICK McKENZIE

Retreat to Boston

After the battles of Lexington and Concord, the British regiments, outnumbered and suffering casualties, retreated back toward Boston. Meanwhile, news of the colonial stand had reached Boston, and a relief column of British troops set out to aid their comrades. Lord Hugh Percy was placed in charge of this relief force. Percy and his men reached the fleeing British at Lexington. The fresh troops kept up an active defense as colonial militiamen—scattered through the surrounding forests and hills—continued to fire into the retreating column. Although Percy's men kept the colonial militia at bay, the rebels managed to harass the British along the entire route to Boston.

Frederick McKenzie was a lieutenant in the Royal Welsh Fusiliers, one of Percy's regiments. In his diary he recalled the tiring march and the menace of colonial snipers hidden in the surrounding woods and farmhouses. He even remembers the taunts of the rebel pursuers who proclaimed their loyalty to patriot leader John Hancock over King George III.

D uring the whole of the march from Lexington, the Rebels kept an incessant irregular fire from all points on the column. . . . Our men had very few opportunities of getting good shots at the Rebels, as they hardly ever fired but under cover of some stone wall, from behind a tree, or out of a house; and the moment they had fired they lay down out of sight until they had loaded again, or the column had passed. In the road indeed in our rear, they were most numerous and came on pretty close, frequently calling out, "King Hancock forever."

Many of them were killed in the houses on the road side from whence they fired; in some, seven or eight men were destroyed. Some houses were forced open in which no person could be discovered, but when the column had passed, numbers sallied forth from some place in which they had lain concealed, fired at the rear guard, and augmented the numbers which followed us. If we had had time to set fire to those houses, many rebels must have perished in

As they retreated to Boston after the battles at Lexington and Concord, British soldiers came under the fire of colonial snipers.

them, but as night drew on, Lord Percy thought it best to continue the march. Many houses were plundered by the soldiers, notwithstanding the efforts of the officers to prevent it. I have no doubt that this inflamed the Rebels, and made many of them follow us farther than they otherwise would have done. By all accounts some soldiers who stayed too long in the houses, were killed in the very act of plundering by those who lay concealed in them.

Allen French, ed., *Diary of Frederick McKenzie: Giving a Daily Narrative of His Military Service as an Officer in the Regiment of Royal Welch Fusiliers During the Years 1775–1781 in Massachusetts, Rhode Island and New York.* Vol. 1. Cambridge, MA: Harvard University Press, 1930.

ANONYMOUS BRITISH SURGEON

Touring a Rebel Camp

At the beginning of the Revolution, the colonial forces did not constitute a professional army. They were a collection of state militias—a band of citizens who typically owned some type of firearm and who volunteered to defend local communities against Indian raids. The militias had no common uniform, no standardized musket, and very little military training. Although many of these men were eager to fight, they usually lacked competent leaders and often had no previous combat experience. They, therefore, could rarely stand up to the well-organized, harshly disciplined, and ably led British army. Still, the militia units remained a large and important part of the newly formed American army. The following description of a typical rebel camp comes from a letter written on May 26, 1775, by a British surgeon who, because of his useful profession, was able to pass from Boston into the rebel lines surrounding the city. Although the tone of the writing is biased, the observations are probably accurate.

Their camp and quarters are plentifully supplied with all sorts of provisions, and the roads are crouded with carts and carriages, bringing them rum, cyder, etc., from the neighbouring towns, for without New-England rum, a New-England army could not be kept together; they could neither fight nor say their prayers, one with another; they drink at least a bottle of it a man a day. . . .

This army, which you will hear so much said, and see so much wrote about, is truly nothing but a drunken, canting, lying, praying, hypocritical rabble, without order, subjection, discipline, or cleanliness; and must fall to pieces of itself in the course of three months, notwithstanding every endeavour of their leaders, teachers, and preachers, though the last are the most canting, hypocritical, lying scoundrels that this or any other country ever afforded.

Margaret Wheeler Willard, ed., *Letters of the American Revolution, 1774–1776*. Boston: Houghton Mifflin, 1925.

Glossary

- **canting:** whining

ANONYMOUS PATRIOT

The Battle of Bunker Hill

After the retreat from Lexington and Concord, the British stayed within the protective limits of Boston. Hoping to trap the British forces, patriot leaders seized the high ground north of the city and planned to place cannons there to shell the enemy. The British governor and general, Thomas Gage, needed to be rid of this threat. In May 1775, Gage received reinforcements from Britain, and he instructed his new generals to devise a plan of attack against the rebel defenses on the nearest hills across the Charles River.

The British won the Battle of Bunker Hill, but almost half of their soldiers had been wounded.

Early in the morning of June 17, 1775, British ships anchored in the river opened fire on rebel trenches and wooden barricades on Breed's Hill. General William Howe was given the task of leading the British infantry on a frontal assault against these positions, but his advance was delayed until late in the afternoon. Around three o'clock, Howe's men—stretched out in battle lines—began their slow march up the hill. Companies of militiamen under Israel Putnam and Joseph Warren poured fire into the wave of oncoming British. Howe was forced to retreat. He advanced a second time, and was likewise repulsed. By then, the colonials were running short of ammunition. They loaded their muskets with anything they could find, including scrap iron and nails. On Howe's third attempt, his infantry routed the patriots. The British had won a costly victory, though. Of the 2,400 British soldiers engaged, 1,054—including 92 officers—had been shot, and 226 of those had been killed. An anonymous militia leader wrote the following letter to a friend in England nine days after the battle. The unknown patriot describes the epic assault on Breed's Hill, which, because of its nearness to a grander hill, is remembered in history books as the Battle of Bunker Hill.

Four thousand men commanded by General Putnam, and led on by Dr. Warren, having prepared every thing for the operation as well as could be contrived or collected were stationed under a half unfinished breastwork and some palisadoes fixed in a hurry. When the enemy were landed, to the number of 2500 . . . and commanded by the most gallant and experienced officers of the last war, they marched to engage 3000 provincials, arrayed in red worsted caps and blue great coats, with guns of different sizes, few of which had bayonets, ill-served artillery, but of invincible courage! The fire from the ships and artillery of the enemy was horrid and amazing; the first onset of the soldiers was bold and fierce, but they were received with equal courage; at length the 38th Regiment gave way, and the rest recoiled. The King's troops were commanded by General Howe. . . . He marched with undaunted spirit at the head of his men; most of his followers were killed round his own person. The King's troops about this time got into much confusion and retreated, but were rallied by the reproaches of General Howe, and the

activity of General Clinton who then joined the battle. The King's troops again made their push against Charlestown, which was then set on fire by them. Our right flank being then uncovered, two floating batteries coming in by the mill dam to take us in the rear, more troops coming from Boston, and our ammunition being almost expended, General Putnam ordered the troops on the left to retreat. The confusion was great for twenty minutes, but in less than half an hour we fell into complete order; the regulars were so mauled they durst not pursue us 200 yards, but almost the last shot they fired killed good Dr. Warren, who had . . . distinguished himself by unparalleled acts of bravery during the whole action, but particularly in covering the retreat. He was a man of great courage, universal learning and much humanity. It may well be said he is the greatest loss we have sustained. General Putnam, at the age of 60, was as active as the youngest officer in the field. We have lost 104 killed, and 306 wounded; a Lieutenant Colonel and 30 men are prisoners, and we anxiously wait their fate. We lost before the action began 18 men by the fire of the ships and the battery from Boston, burying them before the assault. The number of the King's troops killed and wounded are three times our loss.

A leader of the provincial forces, letter regarding the Battle of Bunker Hill, June 26, 1775.

ANONYMOUS BRITISH OFFICER

Routing the Colonials at Long Island

Early in 1776, England's general William Howe led military operations in the Hudson River Valley. As part of his plan to seize the important waterways in the region, Howe wanted to capture the town of New York. To counter this threat, George Washington, the relatively new leader of the colonial forces, decided to fortify the town and neighboring Long Island.

Because Washington was away with other forces, he placed General Israel Putnam in charge of Long Island's defense. Putnam had perhaps ten thousand men to stand off the British invasion. Most were untrained militia whom many colonial officers feared would run from the face of battle unless well protected. So throughout August 1776, the colonial forces built strong fortifications that fronted the entrance to New York harbor.

On August 26, Howe began his assault on New York and Long Island. Because he had suffered great losses in the frontal attack during the Battle of Bunker Hill, Howe was not willing to risk another disaster. Instead of approaching the colonial defenses head on, he sent his army—primarily composed of Hessian mercenaries— to flank, or circle around, the enemy positions. The assault was successful, and the untrained colonials broke and ran after losing about one thousand men. The following letter from a British field officer to his wife attests to Howe's stunning victory. Yet despite his initial success in driving the rebels from their fortifications, Howe failed to pursue and destroy the routed enemy. Washington capitalized on Howe's hesitancy and directed an orderly retreat across the East River to New York, which saved the remnants of the colonial army.

We have had a glorious day against the rebels. We landed on this island the 22d, and that day marched toward Brookland Ferry, opposite New York, where this island is separated from the town by the East River, which is about three quarters of a mile over. . . .

It was not till eight o'clock at night on the 26th that we received our orders to attack, and at eleven the whole army was in motion. The reserve, commanded by Lord Cornwallis, the first brigade of which our regiment makes a part, and the light infantry of the army, the whole under the command of General Clinton, marched by

Colonial forces retreated from the Battle of Long Island after their defeat by the British.

the right. The road to the right, after a march of about seven miles, brought us to an easy and undefended ascent of the hills, which we possessed at daybreak, and continued our rout, gained the rear of the rebels: and while the Hessians and the rest of the army amused them in front and on the left, the grenadiers and light infantry attacked them in the rear: by this masterly maneuver the rebels were immediately thrown into general confusion, and behaved most shamefully. The numbers killed, wounded, and taken you will see in the Gazette. Some of the Hessians told me they had buried between 400 and 500 in one pit.

Such has been their panic that, on the 30th at night, they evacuated their redoubts and entrenchments, which they had retired to, on Brookland Heights, leaving us in possession of this island, which entirely commands New York. Had the works at Brookland been properly defended our motions must have been retarded least three weeks. For my part I think matters will soon be brought to an issue.

Anonymous British field officer, letter to his wife describing the Battle of Long Island, September 1, 1776.

Glossary

- **Brookland:** Brooklyn
- **amused:** occupied
- **grenadiers:** elite soldiers
- **redoubts:** earthen defenses
- **works:** defenses
- **retarded:** held up
- **issue:** end

JABEZ FITCH

A Colonial Prisoner of War

Both British and American prisoners of war were held in any available facility, including ships like the one depicted in this engraving.

British and American prisoners of war during the Revolution spun various tales of appalling living conditions and harsh treatment. Neither side was well equipped to contend with prisoners taken on the battlefield, so treatment of captured soldiers was likely influenced by the temperament of their captors and the available facilities for housing and feeding prisoners. Some American prisoners, such as Jabez Fitch, argued that the fairness of their treatment depended upon whether they were captured by the British or by their German mercenaries. In the following account, Fitch, a colonial soldier captured after the Battle of Long Island in 1776, recalls falling into the hands of British soldiers from the 57th Regiment, a subsequent march past brigades of jeering mercenaries from the German principality of Hesse-Cassel, and finally his temporary detention in a British encampment.

It ought to be mention'd, to the Honour of some . . . who treated us with humanity, & Endeavoured to protect us from the Insults of others; I myself was so happy, as to fall at first into the hands of a party of this kind when taken prisoner; It was part of the 57th: Regt: who used me with some degree of Civility, alth'o some perticular Offrs: were very liberal of their favourite Term (Rebel) & now & then did not forget to Remind me of a halter &c; they did not Rob or Strip me of any of my Clothing but took only my Arms & Ammunition, &; after keeping me in the Field some time, in confinement with several others, under a strong Guard, was sent off to Genll: Grant's Quarters, at Gowaynas.

In this March we pass'd through the Front of several gaids of Hessians . . . they Indeed made a very Warlike appearance, & as no power appear'd at that time to oppose them, their whole Attention seemed to be fixed on us, nor were they by any means sparing of their Insults. . . . Having pass'd through those savage Insults, we at length came onto a hill nigh to the place where we at first Engaged the Enimy in the Morning; we were here met by a number of Insolent Soldiers, among whom was one Woman who appear'd remarkably Malicious and attempted several times, to throw Stones at us, when one of our Guard Inform'd me that her Husband had been kill'd in this Day's Action; We were then conducted down to a Barn, near the water side, where we were drove into a Yard among a great number of Offrs: & men who had been taken before us; soon after we came here, Capt: Jewett with a number of others, were brought in, & confin'd with us; Capt: Jewett had Recd: two Wounds with a Bayonet after he was taken, & Strip'd of his Arms & part of his Clothes, one in the Brest & the other in the Belly, of which he Languished with great pain untill the thirdsday following when he Died; Sargt: Graves was also Stab'd in the Thigh with a Bayonet, after he was taken with Capt: Jewett, of which wound he recovered, alth'o he afterward perish'd in Prison with many hundred others at N. York.

W.H.W. Sabine, ed., *The New York Diary of Lieutenant Jabez Fitch of the 17th(Connecticut) Regiment from August 22, 1776 to December 15, 1777.* New York: Colburn & Tegg, 1954.

Glossary

- **used:** treated
- **Offrs:** officers
- **were very liberal of:** frequently used
- **Remind me of a halter:** pull on his restraints to remind him that he was a prisoner
- **Arms:** weapons
- **Genll:** general
- **gaids:** brigades
- **nigh:** near
- **Enimy:** enemy
- **Malicious:** wicked
- **Bayonet:** blade attached to a musket
- **Languished:** suffered
- **thirdsday:** Thursday

WILLIAM SMALLWOOD

The Unfortunate Suffering of the Sick and Wounded

The American colonies were unprepared for the war that came in 1775. Colonial leaders scrambled to obtain firearms, ammunition, black powder, clothing, and food to send men into battle. The military was perhaps even more ill equipped to take care of wounded soldiers after battle. The Continental Congress tried to address this matter early on, but the lack of medical supplies, qualified doctors, and hospitals meant that field surgeons often petitioned the legislature in vain. Once the Congress proved powerless, medical officers often turned to state or local authorities, usually with similar results.

In the following letter to the Maryland Council of Safety, Colonel William Smallwood of a Maryland regiment complains about the lack of care for the sick and wounded in the 1776 campaigns around New York. Smallwood's letter reveals not only the persistent concern about the lack of medicine and adequate housing for the wounded, but also the difficulties in dealing with the governmental hierarchy that managed the distribution of supplies.

Glossary

- **want:** lack
- **salutary:** beneficial
- **remiss:** negligent
- **fare:** food
- **good-seasoned:** experienced
- **exclusive of which:** besides which

We want medicine much; none can be had here. Our sick have been and are now suffering extremely. The number you'll observe from the list is very considerable, owing in a great measure to the bad provision made for and care taken of them, the men being often moved, and have been exposed to lie on the cold ground ever since they came here; often lying without their tents for several nights, as is now the case, having been five nights and days without them. . . .

Our next greatest suffering proceeds from the great neglect of the sick; and his [Washington's] orders . . . are most salutary, were they to be duly attended to; but here, too, there is not only a shameful but even an inhuman neglect daily

This painting depicts George Washington's visit to wounded soldiers. Lack of medical supplies and doctors made it difficult for the colonial military to take care of its wounded.

exhibited. The Directors of the General Hospitals supply and provide for the sick, [but they] are extremely remiss and inattentive to the well-being and comfort of these unhappy men. . . . I have withdrawn all [my patients from their care] long ago, and had them placed in a comfortable house in the country, and supplied with only the common rations; even this is preferable to the fare of a General Hospital. Two of these Regimental Hospitals, after I have had them put in order, one has been taken away by the Directors for a General Hospital, and my people turned out of doors, and the other would have been taken in the same manner, had I not have applied to General Washington, who told me to keep it. The misfortune is that every supply to the Regimental Hospital of necessaries suitable for the sick must come from an order from these Directors, and is very seldom obtained. . . .

I foresee the evils arising from the shameful neglect in this department. One good-seasoned and well-trained soldier, recovered to health, is worth a dozen new recruits, and is often easier recovered than to get a recruit, exclusive of which this neglect is very discouraging to the soldiery and must injure the service upon the new inlistments after the troops go into winter quarters.

Peter Force, ed., *American Archives: Fifth Series, Containing a Documentary History of the United States of America from the Declaration of Independence, July 4, 1776, to the Definitive Treaty of Peace with Great Britain, September 3, 1783.* Washington: M. St. Clair Clarke and Peter Force, 1848–1853.

ANONYMOUS FRENCH OFFICER

Serving with the Americans

Just after the Revolutionary War began, America was in need of a foreign ally. It logically looked to France, the age-old rival of England. France was eager to aid the rebellion, but it was not immediately willing to declare war on England. Still, the French sent secret stores of weapons and money to the young American government, and many French military officers volunteered to help train the Continental army. The army they found in America, however, was nothing like the ones they were accustomed to in Europe. The colonials had spirit, but they lacked standard-issue uniforms and weapons, and they had no knowledge of battlefield tactics. In the following letter, a French officer describes the advantages and disadvantages of the colonial forces. Of prime concern in his assessment is the Americans' inability to stand up to the ferocious British bayonet charge. The officer concludes that without bayonets of their own—and the training to use them properly—the Continentals will likely continue to flee before the well-executed British charge.

Glossary

- **ascribed:** attributed
- **bayonet:** blade attached to the end of a musket
- **dexterity:** skill
- **firm:** courageous
- **universal prejudice:** widespread preference
- **served his apprenticeship:** trained

The principal advantage of General Howe's army over General Washington's . . . must be ascribed to their being more trained to the use of the bayonet. The American army know their superior dexterity in firing well, and rely entirely upon it. The British Army know it likewise, and dread it. Hence in all engagements the British soldiers rush on with the bayonet after one fire, and seldom fail of throwing the Americans into confusion. Habit, which forms men to do anything, I am persuaded would soon render these brave people. . . . firm at the approaches of a bayonet. . . . General [Charles] Lee, I am told, took great pains to eradicate the universal prejudice he found among the Americans, in favor of terminating the war with fire arms alone. "We must learn to face our enemies," said he, "man to man in the open field, or we shall

Accustomed to their own well-equipped armies, French military officers (pictured) were surprised that the American soldiers lacked uniforms, muskets, and bayonets.

never beat them." The late General [Richard] Montgomery, who served his apprenticeship in the British Army, knew so well that nothing but the bayonet would ever rout troops that had been trained to it, that he once proposed . . . that directions should be given, both in Europe and in this country, to make all muskets intended for the American soldiers two inches longer than the muskets now in use in the British Army, in order that they may have an advantage of their enemy, in charge with bayonets, for, he said, "Britain will never yield but to the push of the bayonet."

Anonymous French officer, letter regarding his service with the Americans, ca. 1777.

JOHN GLOVER

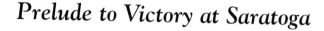

Prelude to Victory at Saratoga

In June 1777, British troops under General John Burgoyne set out on a long trek from Canada with the intention of reaching Albany, New York. American militia and Continental regulars met them at every stage of their progress southward. Burgoyne was able to overcome the rebels and seize several important forts along the route, but each battle drained him of men and supplies. Meanwhile, the delays allowed more colonial forces to gather. Burgoyne's successes prompted the Continental Congress to promote Horatio Gates to overall command of the colonial units in the region on August 19. Gates was determined to keep Burgoyne from reaching his objective. As Burgoyne crossed the Hudson River with his six thousand men—who by now were in desperate need of supplies—Gates had his men positioned behind fortifications on Bemis Heights, a few miles north of Saratoga, New York.

Burgoyne pushed into the weak American left flank at a place called Freeman's Farm on September 19. Benedict Arnold, a subordinate American commander, foresaw the danger and rallied troops to stem the British attack. During the firefight at Freeman's Farm, the British lost about six hundred men, compared to three hundred colonial casualties. In the following letter, John Glover, a colonial participant in the Battle of Freeman's Farm, relates to a relative the effect of the losses on both the colonial and British armies.

Since my last letter to you we have had two flags of truce from the enemy, by which we have received an account of their killed and wounded in the battle of the 19th, 746, among which is a great proportion of officers. But the truth has not come out yet, as I'm fully persuaded, & it's the opinion of all the Gen. Officers, that they must have suffered a great many more. . . .

We had 81 officers and men killed dead on the spot and 202 wounded, many of which are since dead, in the whole 303—a very inconsiderable number, when we consider how hot the battle was & how long it continued, being 6 hours without any intermission, saving about half an hour between 2 and 3 o'clock.

The enemy have remained very quiet ever since at about one mile distance, not attempting to advance one step. We are continually harrassing them by driving their pickets, bringing off their horses.

We have taken 30 prisoners since the battle, and as many more deserted.

Our men are in fine spirits, are very bold and daring, a proof of which I will give you in an instance two nights past.

Although British general John Burgoyne seized several important forts between Canada and Albany, he surrendered to colonial forces after the battle at Saratoga.

I ordered 100 men from my Brigade to take off a picket of about 60 of the enemy, who were posted about half a mile from me, at the same time ordered a covering party of 200 to support them. This being the first enterprise of this kind, & as it was proposed by me, I was very anxious for its success. I therefore went myself. The night being very foggy and dark, could not find the enemy till after day. When I made the proper disposition for the attack, they went on like so many tigers, bidding defiance to musket balls and bayonets. Drove the enemy, killed 3, and wounded a great number more, took one prisoner, 8 Packs, 8 Blankets, 2 guns, 1 sword, and many other articles of Plunder without any loss on our side.

Matters can't remain long as they now are. Burgoyne has only 20 days provision. He must give us battle in a day or two, or else retire back.

John Glover, letter to Jonathan Glover and Azor Orne, September 29, 1777, in *Historical Collections of the Essex Institute*. Vol. 5. Salem, MA: G.M. Whipple; A.A. Smith, 1863.

Glossary

- **intermission:** break; pause
- **saving:** except for
- **pickets:** sentries
- **disposition:** placement of troops
- **Plunder:** loot
- **provision:** food

ALBIGENCE WALDO

Winter at Valley Forge

After the British captured Philadelphia in September 1777, they engaged in a few skirmishes with George Washington's army but retired to the city to wait out the winter. Washington bottled up Philadelphia, but could not lay an effective siege. He retired his army to winter quarters at Valley Forge, Pennsylvania. By the end of 1777, many of his militia had deserted him to return to their homes. The remnants braved freezing cold at a camp without adequate shelter or provisions. Many of the soldiers had worn through their shoes in months of marching and were forced to wrap their feet in linen to withstand the chill.

Albigence Waldo was a colonial soldier in Washington's camp. In this excerpt from his diary, Waldo speaks of his own fatigue and sickness as well as the general sufferings of all those who waited out the bitterly cold months at Valley Forge.

Glossary

- **hitherto:** until now
- **Alacrity:** eagerness
- **Cloaths:** clothes
- **smoak'd:** smoked
- **Felicities:** comforts
- **pox:** curse
- **Hector:** tough bully
- **Melanchollic:** melancholic, sorrowful
- **extolling:** praising
- **harkee:** take heed
- **Constitution:** will
- **habitations:** homes

December 14—Prisoners & Deserters are continually coming in. The Army which has been surprisingly healthy hitherto, now begins to grow sickly from the continued fatigues they have suffered this Campaign. Yet they still show a spirit of Alacrity & Contentment not to be expected from so young Troops. I am Sick—discontented—and out of humour. Poor food—hard lodging—Cold Weather—fatigue—Nasty Cloaths—nasty Cookery—Vomit half my time—smoak'd out of my senses—the Devil's in't—I can't Endure it—Why are we sent here to starve and Freeze—What sweet Felicities have I left at home; A charming Wife—pretty Children—Good Beds—good food—good Cookery—all agreeable—all harmonious. Here all Confusion—smoke & Cold—hunger & filthyness—A pox on my bad luck. There comes a bowl of beef soup-full of burnt leaves and dirt, sickish enough to make a Hector spue—away with it Boys—I'll live like the

Chameleon upon Air. Poh! Poh! crys Patience within me—you talk like a fool. Your being sick Covers your mind with a Melanchollic Gloom, which makes every thing about you appear gloomy. See the poor Soldier, when in health—with what cheerfulness he meets his foes and encounters every hardship—if barefoot, he labours thro' the Mud & Cold with a Song in his mouth extolling War & Washington—if his food be bad, he

Many colonial soldiers at Valley Forge had to wrap their feet in linen because they had worn out their shoes.

eats it notwithstanding with seeming content—blesses God for a good Stomach and Whistles it into digestion. But harkee Patience, a moment—There comes a Soldier, his bare feet are seen thro' his worn out Shoes, his legs nearly naked from the tatter'd remains of an only pair of stockings, his Breeches not sufficient to cover his nakedness, his Shirt hanging in Strings, his hair dishevell'd, his face meagre; his whole appearance pictures a person forsaken & discouraged. He comes, and crys with an air of wretchedness & despair, I am Sick my feet lame, my legs are sore, my body cover'd with this tormenting Itch—my Cloaths are worn out, my Constitution is broken, my former Activity is exhausted by fatigue, hunger & Cold, I fail fast I shall soon be no more! and all the reward I shall get will be—"Poor Will is dead." People who live at home in Luxury and Ease, quietly possessing their habitations, Enjoying their Wives & families in peace, have but a very faint Idea of the unpleasing sensations, and continual Anxiety the Man endures who is in a Camp, and is the husband and parent of an agreeable family. These same People are willing we should suffer every thing for their Benefit & advantage, and yet are the first to Condemn us for not doing more!!

Albigence Waldo, diary, December 11–29, 1777. *Pennsylvania Magazine of History and Biography.* Vol. 21. Philadelphia: Historical Society of Pennsylvania, 1897.

ROBERT BROWNSFIELD

Tarleton's Quarter

Much of the combat in the southern colonies during the Revolution was character-ized by small skirmishes between community militias, some loyal to the Crown and some in favor of independence. The loyalists were well organized in the South, and they bested the rebels in many battles. One of the most infamous of their units was the Loyal Legion, a combined force of veteran loyalists and expert British cavalry. Formed in 1778, the Loyal Legion was commanded by a dashing horseman named Banastre Tarleton. The unit won stunning victories at Moncks Corner and Lenud's Ferry while campaigning in South Carolina. On May 29, 1780, however, reputa-tion of the Loyal Legion and its commander was forever tainted.

At Waxhaw Creek, close to the Virginia border, the Loyal Legion intercepted a unit of 350 Virginia militia commanded by Colonel Abraham Buford. Falling upon the enemy's rear guard, Tarleton's men surprised the patriots. After a brief show of force, Buford asked that a white flag be hoisted to signal the militia's surrender. In the next few confusing moments, the flag bearer was shot down, and the militiamen who had already dropped their weapons expecting quarter—or mercy—were speared by the bayonets of the British and loyalist soldiers who stood guard. The massacre that followed was, by most colonial accounts, quite savage. It gave rise to the popular colonial expression "Tarleton's quarter," meaning no mercy is expected for those who surrender. One account of the incident was provided by Robert Brownsfield, a physician who survived the tragedy.

Buford, now perceiving that further resistance was hopeless, ordered a flag to be hoisted and the arms to be grounded, expecting the usual treatment sanctioned by civilized warfare. This, however, made no part of Tarleton's creed. His ostensible pretext for the relentless barbarity that ensued was that his horse was killed under him just as the flag was raised. He affected to believe that this was done afterwards, and imputed it to treachery on the part of Buford; but, in reality, a safe opportunity was presented to gratify that thirst for blood which marked his character in every conjuncture that promised probable impunity to himself. Ensign Cruit, who advanced the flag, was instantly cut down.

Viewing this as an earnest of what they were to expect, a resumption of their arms was attempted . . . but before this was fully effected, Tarleton with his cruel myrmi-

Banastre Tarleton
commanded the
Loyal Legion, a
southern militia
unit made up of
loyalists and British
cavalrymen.

Tarleton's Loyal Legion gained infamy when they massacred hundreds of Virginia patriots on May 29, 1780.

dons was in the midst of them, when commenced a scene of indiscriminate carnage never surpassed by the ruthless atrocities of the most barbarous savages.

The demand for quarter, seldom refused to a vanquished foe, was at once found to be in vain; not a man was spared, and it was the concurrent testimony of all the survivors that for fifteen minutes after every man was prostrate they went over the ground plunging their bayonets into every one that exhibited any signs of life, and in some instances, where several had fallen one over the other, these monsters were seen to throw off on the point of the bayonet the uppermost, to come at those beneath.

William Dobein James, *A Sketch of the Life of Brig. Gen. Francis Marion and a History of His Brigade.* Charleston, SC: Gould and Milet, 1821.

Glossary

- **ostensible pretext:** excuse
- **imputed it to:** blamed it on
- **conjuncture:** situation
- **impunity:** escape from punishment
- **myrmidons:** loyal followers
- **earnest:** sign
- **prostrate:** lying on the ground
- **bayonets:** blades attached to muskets

FOR MORE INFORMATION

Books

Clinton Cox, *Come All You Brave Soldiers: Blacks in the Revolutionary War*. New York: Scholastic, 1995.

Richard Ferrie, *The World Turned Upside Down: George Washington and the Battle of Yorktown*. Bridgewater, NJ: Holiday House, 1999.

Jim Murphy, *A Young Patriot: The American Revolution as Experienced by One Boy*. New York: Houghton Mifflin, 1998.

R. Conrad Stein, *Valley Forge*. San Francisco: Childrens, 1999.

Gail B. Stewart, *Life of a Soldier in Washington's Army*. San Diego: Lucent, 2002.

Web Sites

The History Place: The American Revolution
www.historyplace.com
One of the many topics covered by The History Place Web site, this series of pages on the Revolution presents time lines of the era. On each time line page, visitors can access information that relates to the period between early colonization and 1790.

Kid Info: American Revolution
www.kidinfo.com
This Web site gathers links to other sites devoted to some aspect of the Revolution. This is a good place to track down further information on a specific topic of interest.

Liberty: The American Revolution
www.pbs.org
A companion to the PBS documentary miniseries on the Revolution, this Web site is an excellent resource for students.

INDEX